THE CONCEPT OF EDUCATION IN ISLAM

A FRAMEWORK FOR AN ISLAMIC PHILOSOPHY OF EDUCATION

SYED MUHAMMAD NAQUIB AL-ATTAS

Qadeem PRESS

THE CONCEPT OF EDUCATION IN ISLAM

A FRAMEWORK FOR AN ISLAMIC PHILOSOPHY OF EDUCATION

SYED MUHAMMAD NAQUIB AL-ATTAS

M.A (McGill), Ph.D (london)
University Professor of Islamic Thought and Civilization: Founder Director
International Institute of Islamic Thought and Civilization: First Holder of the Distinguished al-Ghazali Chair of Islamic Thought

FIRST PUBLISHED BY THE MUSLIM YOUTH MOVEMENT OF MALAYSIA (ABIM), 1980
SECOND IMPRESSION BY THE INTERNATIONAL INSTITUTE OF
ISLAMIC THOUGHT AND CIVILIZATION (ISTAC) 1991;
THIRD IMPRESSION BY THE INTERNATIONAL INSTITUTE OF
ISLAMIC THOUGHT AND CIVILIZATION (ISTAC) 1999.
205A JALAN DAMANSARA, DAMANSARA HEIGHTS,
50480 KUALA LUMPUR
Tel: 603-254 4444 Fax: 603-254 8343 E-Mail: istac@po.jaring.my

CONTENTS

AUTHOR'S NOTE

The present book is a commentary of what is contained in pages 4–7, 9–12 and 14–20 of my paper entitled: *Preliminary Thoughts on the Nature of Knowledge and the Definition and Aims of Education,* presented at the First World Conference on Muslim Education held at Mecca from March 31 to April 8 in 1977.[1] Since this book is an elaboration which seeks to clarify the subject of the paper cited above, and is naturally connected in logical sequence with the ideas conveyed therein as a development of its basic concepts, the substance of this book was appropriately presented as a paper to the Second World Conference on Muslim Education held at Islamabad from March 15 to March 20 this year.[2]

It is basically a book of definitions relating to the essential elements in the concept of education and the educational process as envisaged in Islam. In the concluding remarks of the paper

---

1 Organized by King Abdulaziz University, Makkah al-Mukarramah, Saudi Arabia. The paper was published in English and Arabic by the Conference as a key paper of the Conference, and it was read in the Plenary Session II on April 3,1977 (see the *Conference Book,* King Abdulaziz University, Jeddah & Mecca al-Mukarramah, 1397/1977, 35 and 37). It was subsequently published, together with seven selected papers, as a book under the title: *Aims and Objectives of Islamic Education,* ed. Syed Muhammad al-Naquib al-Attas, Hodder and Stoughton (London) and King Abdulaziz University (Jeddah), 1979. The reference above to pages 4–7, 9–12 and 14–20 in the paper corresponds with pages 23–27, 29–33 and 35–42 of the book cited. The paper was also published, with some modifications and additions, as a chapter under the heading: 'The Dewesternization of Knowledge' in my book, *Islām and Secularism* (ABIM, Kuala Lumpur, 1978, V, 127–160).

2 Organized by Quaid-i-Azam University in collaboration with King Abdulaziz University (Jeddah) at Islamabad, Pakistan. The paper was published in the proceedings of the Conference.

cited above, I stated on page 21 that the essential elements of the Islamic system of education are based on certain key concepts, namely: the concept of religion *(dīn)*; the concept of man *(insān)*; the concept of knowledge *(ʻilm* and *maʻrifah)*; the concept of wisdom *(ḥikmah)*; the concept of justice *(ʻadl)*; the concept of right action *(ʻamal* as *adab)*; and the concept of the university *(kulliyyah—jāmiʻah)*. Here in this book I treat these concepts again, dispensing with the need for further clarification on those that were already clarified in the paper.[3] The definitions demonstrate the interrelated nature of the concepts. The concept of *adab* as right action or discipline is here elaborated; new definitions are added, such as those of the intellect *(ʻaql)* and what constitutes rationality *(nuṭq)*; of islamization of language and of thought; of meaning *(maʻnā)*, knowledge and education *(ta'dīb)*. These definitions are based on personal reflection and conceptual analysis viewed in the context of the Islamic intellectual and religious tradition. With the exception perhaps of the concept of justice,[4] the definitions are original and, to the best of my knowledge, they are also new; born as they are out of the present need for creative thinking and clarification of the basic concepts pertaining to knowledge and education. Moreover, the formulation of these key concepts and the way they are brought together in meaningful pattern, both in the paper and in this book, are perhaps the first formulation and conceptualization of its kind found in the context of Muslim intellectual and religious thinking of our times.

---

3 For an elaboration of the concept of religion and related concepts, my book, *Islām: the Concept of Religion and the Foundation of Ethics and Morality,* ABIM, Kuala Lumpur, 1976, is referred.

4 The concept of justice which I have formulated here and in earlier writings (the paper cited in note 1 and the book in note 3 above), although original in its conception, is somewhat similar to that conceived by the early Ṣūfis. See, for example, al-Hujwīrī's *Kashf al-Maḥjūb,* tr. R. A. Nicholson, E. J. W. Gibb Memorial, vol. XVII, Leyden & London, 1911, 387, where *'adl* is defined as 'putting everything in its proper place.'

Already in the paper I have put forward some new ideas: the idea that the purpose of seeking knowledge and of education in Islam is to produce a good man and not a good citizen; the meaning of the concept 'good' in the definition of good man; the concept of the Islamic university as reflecting man, i.e., the Universal or Perfect Man, and not the state—which is not to be confused with what many Muslims today think of as an 'Islamic university'. Now in this little book I present some other new ideas: the concept of methodology of scientific research and study of nature along the lines of Quranic interpretation *(tafsīr* and *ta'wīl)*; the concept of Islamic language; the role of the Holy Qur'ān in the islamization of the languages of Muslim peoples including the Arabic language; finally, that education and the educational process in the Islamic sense is in reality defined by the concept of *ta'dīb* and not by that of *tarbiyah*.

I make no apology for making claims to originality in the conception of new ideas and definitions as specified and formulated herein and in my earlier writings, because the necessity for such claims has now arisen. I refer here to the regrettable instances in which certain Muslim scholars of Islam and scholars and intellectuals among the Muslims have appropriated some of these ideas in their writings without due acknowledgement after they had become acquainted with them in lectures, conferences, meetings and private discussions. The purpose of acknowledging the source of an important idea is—apart from the moral obligation to do so—to point those who pursue the subject for the sake of the Community to the right direction; so that they might not be misled concerning the value and validity of that idea, and its further development and clarification along logical lines which only the original source is justly capable of doing. But if Muslim writers, whether in English, Arabic, or other languages, are in the habit of either pointing to themselves or to others in respect of significant ideas not really originated by them, then they obliterate thereby the real source and deprive the Community of knowledge of the right direction.

The ideas discussed under each sub-heading in the book can indeed be expanded in further elaboration, and their soundness can be tested and evaluated in accordance with their suitableness to the requirements of the truth as affirmed on the testimony of Islamic sources and reflected in the Islamic intellectual and religious tradition. But the aim of this book is only to provide the necessary framework within which the Islamic philosophy of education can be formulated and conceptualized.

Syed Muhammad Naquib al-Attas
Petaling Jaya
16 *Jumādā al-Akhirah* 1400
1 May 1980

The Concept of Education in Islam

Statement of Intention

I propose at this stage of our deliberations to define education as envisaged in the context of Islam, and to formulate the form of the system of education thus defined, as the nature of education and of its form is in truth not yet realized and is generally unknown among Muslims the world over. Once the definition is clarified and the form known and realized, the formulation of the curricula that would correspond to the requirements of the definition and the form, would be comparatively a less problematic matter.

The form, as I envisage it, is new in the philosophical as well as the physical sense; and because of this, preliminary explanation is necessary before it can be introduced to our understanding, and accepted as one genuinely Islamic in character. In the process of that explanation, I shall have to give background knowledge of the problems that have created our present general crisis in education. These problems pertain to our intellectual history as well as that of Western culture and civilization.

In elaborating on the nature of the educational crisis in which we are presently involved, certain preliminary remarks would suffice to demonstrate the extent to which we have deviated from the Islamic intellectual tradition in the course of our intellectual history. These remarks are meant to remind us of what we have apparently forgotten in the way of methodology and the correct application of linguistic symbols.

The Scientific Nature of the Arabic Language

When we speak of methodology and the correct application of linguistic symbols, our first consideration is to understand the scientific nature of the Arabic language, which is *the* language of Islam, and upon which the Islamic sciences are based, and by which its vision of reality and truth is projected. By 'scientific' I mean the *definitive* aspect that characterizes science, for *science is definition*—both in the sense of *ḥadd (حد)* and *rasm (رسم)—of reality (حقيقة)* . The scientific structure of Arabic is attested to by the mere fact that it is the language in which the Holy Qur'ān is revealed. When God, Glorious and Most Exalted, says that the Holy Qur'ān in Arabic contains no 'crookedness' (قرآنا عربيا غيرذي عوج لعلهم يتقون),[1] what is implied with reference to the language is that since the Holy Qur'ān is the Fountain of true knowledge, the linguistic form through which that knowledge flows and by which it is made to flow, must also be of such a nature that it too is not susceptible of 'crookedness' (عوج)—that is, of deviations from the 'straight' (قيم) course, from the right meanings that convey truth directly, without swerving elsewhere, without distortions. Languages are susceptible of semantic change brought about by the vicissitudes of history and society; and of relative and subjective interpretations in their linguistic symbols. As such language presents no guarantee of scientific precision with respect to meaning; particularly to meanings that convey *absolute* and *objective* truth. With respect to the Arabic language, however, we say that it does not belong to the same category as other languages insofar as its semantic structure is concerned. This is due to the fact that (1) its linguistic structure is established upon a firm system of 'roots'; and that (2) its semantic structure is governed by a clearly defined system of semantic 'fields' that determine the conceptual structures

---

1 39: 28.

inherent in its vocabulary, and that is also fixed permanently by (1) above; and that (3) its words, meanings, grammar and prosody have been scientifically recorded and established so as to maintain semantic permanence. From the earliest periods of Islam, Muslim lexicologists have been extraordinarily aware of the scientific character of the Arabic language, and the Arabs were, to my knowledge, perhaps the first people we know in the history of mankind to seriously compile lexicons pertaining to their language. For an uninterrupted period of over 1000 years, from the time of Ibn 'Abbās down to about 200 years to our present time—that is, to that of Sayyid Murtaḍā al-Zabīdī—learned Muslims have laboured and produced voluminous lexicons, some extending to more than 20 volumes, and some intended to extend to more than 60 volumes, in order to preserve purity and authoritative meaning in Arabic. Ibn 'Abbās himself was the first to effect the evaluation of the method of determining authentic and authoritative meaning, which he initiated in the process of interpretation of the Holy Qur'ān. During his time, then, the process of testing the authenticity of meaning, and of establishing the highest authorities with respect to the words, meanings, grammar, and the prosody of the classical Arabic language, was already underway; and by the second century after the Hijrah, the methodological division into four groups, designed to determine and establish authentic authorities on all aspects of the Arabic language, such as the Jāhilī, the *Mukhaḍram,* the *Islāmī,* and the *Muwallad,* was completed. It was further established among the Arabs themselves that the highest authority relating to all aspects of the Arabic language, with the exception of its prosody, is the Holy Qur'ān, and next after that the *Ḥadīth* of the Holy Prophet, upon whom be peace. Some of the celebrated lexicons that were compiled from the second to the twelfth centuries after the Hijrah include the *Kitāb al-'Ayn* of al-Khalīl (d. 160 A.H.); the *Jamharah* of Ibn Durayd (d. 321); the *Tahdhīb* of al-Azharī (d. 370); the *Muḥīṭ* of Ibn 'Abbād (d. 385); the *Mujmal* of Ibn Fāris (d. 390); the *Ṣiḥāḥ* of al-Jawharī (d. 398); the *Jāmi'* of al-Qazzāz (d. 412); the *Mu'ab* of Ibn Tamām (d. 436); the *Muḥkam* of Ibn Sayyidih (d. 458); the *Asās* of al-Zamakhsharī (d. 538); the

Mughrib of al-Muṭārizī (d. 610); the *'Ubāb* of al-Ṣaghānī (d. 680); the *Lisān al-'Arab* of Ibn Manẓūr (d. 711); the *Tahdhīb al-Tahdhīb* of al-Tanūkhī (d. 723); the *Miṣbāḥ* of al-Fayyūmī (completed 734); the *Mughnī* of Ibn Hishām (d. 761); the *Qāmūs* and the *Lāmi'* of al-Fayrūzābādī (d. 816); and the *Tāj al-'Arūs* of al-Zabīdī (d. 1205). Apart from the brief list of lexicons cited above—lexicons which exhibit the utmost care and painstaking research with which the truly learned men of Islam of past times laboured to produce as works of such erudition, authority, exactness and copiousness never approached in the case of any other language—we might further add dictionaries of technical terms relating to Islamic arts, sciences and metaphysics, notably the *Kitāb al-Ta'rīfāt* of al-Jurjānī (d. 816); and the encyclopaedic *Kashshāf Iṣṭilāḥāt al-Funūn* of al-Tahānawī (written and completed in the 12th century A.H.), containing also explanations in Persian of some of the Arabic terms listed in the work. In all these celebrated works, the records of words and their significations and the manner of their correct usages are set forth in precise and scientific detail, complete with authorities cited in each case.

We mention all this to demonstrate that such exacting and yet prolific efforts recording the meanings and usages of the Arabic-Islamic vocabulary for an uninterrupted period spanning over a thousand years from the earliest periods of Islam is a clear testimony of the scientific nature of that language that defines reality and truth as envisaged in the worldview of Islam in such wise as to guarantee semantic precision and permanence. Indeed, it was because of the scientific nature of the structure of the language that the first science among the Muslims—the science of exegesis and commentary *(tafsīr:* تفسير*)*—became possible and actualized; and the kind of exegesis and commentary not quite identical with the Greek hermeneutics, nor indeed with the hermeneutics of the Christians, nor with any 'science' of interpretation of sacred scripture of any other culture and religion. In *tafsīr,* there is no room for learned guess or conjecture; no room for interpretation based upon subjective readings, or understandings based merely upon the idea of historical relativism as if semantic change had occurred in the conceptual structures of the words and terms that make up the vocabulary of the sacred text. In *tafsīr,* the process of interpretation is based upon the Holy Qur'ān and the *ḥadīth* supported by the knowledge of the semantic 'fields' that govern the conceptual structures of the Quranic vocabulary which projects the Islamic vision of reality and truth. It is therefore based upon *established knowledge* of the 'fields' of meaning as couched in the Arabic language and as organized and applied in the Holy Qur'ān and reflected in the *Ḥadīth* and the Sunnah. *Tafsīr is* a scientific method; and its emphasis upon the condition of established knowledge of the given linguistic symbols and their significations as determined by the semantic contexts approaches the nature of an exact science. When God Most Exalted says that He brings forth the living from the dead (يخرج الحيّ من الميّت),[2] and we interpret it to mean, to give one particular instance, that He brings forth the bird from the egg, this is *tafsīr.* But when we interpret the same passage to mean that He brings forth the believer (المؤمن) from the unbeliever or misbeliever (الكافر), or that He brings forth the knower (العالم) from the ignorant (الجاهل), then this is *ta'wīl (تأويل).*[3] It is clear from this that *ta'wīl* is but an intensive form of *tafsīr;* for while the latter refers to the discovery, detecting or revealing of what is meant by an ambiguous expression, the former refers to what that expression *ultimately* means. Now the discovery, detecting or revealing of the concealed meanings of the words in the above quoted passage—which revolves around the two ambiguous words in question: the living (الحيّ) and the dead (الميّت)—is in both cases of *tafsīr* and *ta'wīl* based on other passages in the Holy Qur'ān which reveal the conceptual structures of those words and the contexts in which they revolve—that is, their semantic 'fields'—and on what is reflected of them in the occasions in which they were revealed and in the *Ḥadīth.* Consider, for example, the *ta'wīl* interpreting the passage as meaning that He brings forth the

---

2 6: 95.

3 Al-Jurjānī's definition based on earlier authorities. See his *Kitāb al-Ta'rīfāt,* 52 (in Flugel's edition, Beirut, 1969).

believer from the unbeliever or misbeliever. In another passage in the Holy Qur'ān, God Most Exalted says that He sends down rain from the skies to revive an earth that is already dead (وما انزل الله من السماء من ماء فاحيا به الأرض بعد موتها). [4] In yet another He says that the skies contain rain (والسماء ذات الرجع).[5] The word *raj'* (رجع), interpreted as rain, signifies something that returns again and again, and that it brings good, as rain returns again and again from the skies by which He brings forth the living plants from an earth that is dead. Now there is a close conceptual connection between the Quranic concept of return or *raj'*, and its concept of din (دين), or true religion; and it is a fact that one of the basic meanings of the term *dīn is* recurrent rain, so that the term rain symbolizes true religion. So Islam, the true religion, is like rain by which He gives life to man who is otherwise dead like the earth. Thus a believer, a man who saturates himself in true religion, is 'living', and an unbeliever or a misbeliever is 'dead'.[6] Alluding to this the Holy Prophet, may God bless and give him peace, said: "The similitude of one who remembers his Lord and one who does not remember his Lord is like the living and the dead" (مثل الذى يذكر ربه والذى لايذكر ربه مثل الحي والميّت). Thus in this way and more, the many and yet relevant significations in the Quranic expressions and in the *Ḥadīth* revolving around the concepts of life and death, and their symbolical references to belief and unbelief, or knowledge and ignorance, is expounded and elaborated in great detail.[7]

---

4 2: 164.

5 86: 11.

6 For a further interpretation of the concept of *dīn*, see my ***Islām: The Concept of Religion and the Foundation of Ethics and Morality***, Kuala Lumpur, 1976.

7 As a further example of what is stated, we may cite the interpretations given by Ibn 'Abbās, 'Ikrimah, Ibn Aslam, al-Ḍahhāk, Abū Sinān and Qatādah on *sūrah* 6:122 as reported and authenticated by al-Suyūṭī in his *Al-Durr al-Manthūr*, 6 vols., Beirut [n.d.], 3: 43–44.

The Semantic Field in the Context of Islam

The substance of what is contained in the foregoing paragraphs serves as an introduction to the central subject of this book: the concepts of knowledge and education in the context of Islam. As will be clearly seen, the relevance obtained between *tafsīr* and *ta'wīl* as valid methods of approach to knowledge and scientific methodology respecting our study of the world of nature is of considerable significance in our conception of knowledge and education. For both the Holy Qur'ān as the Open Book, and the world of nature as another Open Book demand that their Words be interpreted in accordance with the valid methods of *tafsīr* and *ta'wīl* which are unique to Islam. We will return to this important point again in due course. In either case, the right method demands correct application of the linguistic symbols pertaining to Arabic in the context of Islam. The same method applies in all other forms of explicating the meanings of Arabic words and terms, such as in commentary *(sharḥ:* شرح*)* and in any other form of scientific intellectual enquiry and research. The word must be correctly applied within the context of its semantic 'field', its field of meaning that governs its usage, and that bears considerable influence on other fields of meaning that 'overlap' and impinge upon each other. Al-Jāḥiẓ (d. 255) has given us an illuminating example of this in his *Kitāb al-Bukhalā'*, where he discussed the concept of greed, or avarice, or miserliness *(bukhl:* بخل*)*. In defining this concept, he progressively settled the limits within which the word *bakhīl* (بخيل) is generally applied: it is a word that is generally applicable to the animal species; and among the animal species, to man alone; and among mankind, to the male; and among the males, to the mature; and among the mature, to the sane; and among the sane, to the wealthy—and so on. It is clear that we would be violating the conceptual order of the concept *bukhl* if we refer to a poor man or woman or boy as a *bakhīl*. The field of meaning within which is described the conceptual structure symbolized by a central word or term is what we have called here a 'semantic field'; and a semantic field usually overlaps other such fields, so that the inherent conceptual structure is interrelated with other such structures as projected in the Islamic vocabulary which is governed by the Quranic worldview and reflected in the *Ḥadīth* and the Sunnah. By 'Islamic vocabulary' is not meant all the Arabic words arranged in alphabetical order as in a dictionary; it is meant rather to signify all the Arabic terms that are interrelated in meaningful pattern, projecting a worldview that is distinctly Quranic. The Islamic vocabulary comprises a large number of Arabic terms, and among them are a relatively small number of 'key' terms which comprise the Islamic *basic* vocabulary. It is this basic vocabulary that projects a distinctly Islamic worldview in the Muslim mind.

Now the languages of all Muslim peoples have already been infused with this basic vocabulary. The infusion referred to occurred historically with the spread of Islam, and the languages infused with the Islamic basic vocabulary have assimilated it in varying degrees, both of extent and intensity depending upon the cultural and intellectual levels of the speakers, and have made that Islamic basic vocabulary their own basic vocabulary. In this way the non-Arabic languages of Muslim peoples have been 'islamized'. This remarkable and revolutionary phenomenon, which I call the *islamization* of language and which necessarily occurs simultaneously with the islamization of the mind and of the vision of reality and truth as perceived by the mind, is what constitutes the fundamental cultural element in conversion to Islam. Indeed, in this respect, the Arabic language itself has not been exempted from the process of islamization. The lexicologists among the Western orientalists have assumed that at the time of the revelation of the Holy Qur'ān and the advent of Islam among the Arabs, the Arabic language had undergone a rapid process of corruption and decay. The prolific, intellectually and scientifically momentous activity of recording authenticity of meaning and authoritative usage, such as I have briefly mentioned earlier, is interpreted by them as a remarkable step to stem the tide of corruption and decay, and to preserve for posterity what could be preserved. In my own humble estimation, however, what they have portrayed might not be the correct interpretation of the real situation. What had occurred to Arabic with the revelation of the Holy Qur'ān and the advent of Islam among the Arabs was what I have called the islamization of the language. Viewed from the standpoint of those whose standards of purity, authenticity and authoritative usage are measured in terms of Jāhiliyyah Arabic, that revolutionary phenomenon of islamization of the language would of course be seen as a 'corruption' and a 'decay'. The truth was that the revelation of the Holy Qur'ān in Arabic caused a revolution in the language; the Jāhilī mind was engulfed in conceptual upheaval and dissolved in utter disarray by it. The Arabic of the Holy Qur'ān not only sounded strange and yet compellingly magical to him, but it meant drastic change in the familiar mental forms the language once projected to his vision. Although the words cast were the same as he knew them before, yet now they no longer served to describe the semantic fields in the vocabulary known to him. An illuminating example of this is the word *karīm* (كريم), which was a key term in the Jāhilī vocabulary, and which as such meant nobility of lineage which went hand in hand with extravagant generosity. For the Jāhilī, the concept of *karam* (كرم) was very much the contrary of *bukhl* which we mentioned earlier. The Holy Qur'ān , however, altered the semantic field of *karam* as known to the Jāhilī, and made it to revolve around the concept of *taqwā* (تقوى),[8] producing a semantic field altogether unknown to him. The Holy Qur'ān altered the conceptual structures of Jāhilī key terms in such a radical manner as to effect alterations in entire semantic fields in the Jāhilī vocabulary. The conceptual and semantic network that patterned itself into such a vocabulary was itself dissolved forever, in such wise that the worldview it projected was abolished from the Arabic language. Although the words used in the Holy Qur'ān are the same as those used in pre-Islamic times, the concepts they project and the roles they play in the framework of the semantic vocabulary did not evolve from the Jāhilī worldview. The islamization of Arabic, then, consisted in *the Quranic reorganization and reformation of the conceptual structures, semantic fields, vocabulary*

[8] Q.v. 49:13—(إن اكرمكم عندالله أتقاكم)

and basic vocabulary that once served the Jāhilī vision of the world and of life and human existence. The effect of this islamization of the language was reflected in the *Ḥadīth* and the Sunnah; and the resultant usage was recorded with such diligent and penetrating scholarly zeal by learned Muslims gifted with wisdom and insight and discernment. It is this *new* Arabic language which is meant here as the one whose nature is scientific. The same process of islamization was effected in the conceptual and semantic network of the non-Arabic languages of Muslim peoples; and in order that the islamized conceptual and semantic network become an established principle in governing authentic and authoritative meaning and correct usage, as well as in projecting the Islamic worldview, each language of a Muslim people has been infused with the Islamic basic vocabulary. The Islamic basic vocabulary is composed of key terms and concepts (اصطلاحات) related to one another meaningfully and altogether determining the conceptual structure of reality and existence projected by them. In this way, each language of a Muslim people with every other has in common this Islamic basic vocabulary as its own basic vocabulary; and as such all languages of Muslim peoples indeed belong to the same family of Islamic languages. What I wish to introduce here is the concept of *Islamic language*—that there is such a thing as Islamic language. Because language that can be categorized as Islamic does exist in virtue of the common Islamic basic vocabulary inherent in each of them, the key terms and concepts in the basic vocabulary of each of them ought indeed to convey the *same meanings,* since they are all involved in the same conceptual and semantic network. For this reason semantic precision with regard to the application of the Islamic key terms and concepts in our rational and intellectual deliberations is of paramount importance. If, for example, we find today that the word *'ilm (علم),* which is a major key term in the basic vocabulary of all Islamic languages, conveys different connotations in each member of the family of Islamic languages, this regrettable fact is not caused by what is vaguely termed as 'social change'. It is, rather, caused by confusion and ignorance due to loss of *adab*—which I will explain later—which undermines legitimate spiritual and intellectual authority; and to the infusion of alien concepts which cause displacements in the network of semantic fields and conceptual relations. Many major key terms in the Islamic basic vocabulary of the languages of Muslim peoples have now been displaced and made to serve absurdly in alien fields of meaning. This modern cultural phenomenon is what is causing the confusion of the Muslim mind. It is a kind of regression towards non-Islamic worldviews; it is what I call the *deislamization* of language. Ignorance and confusion and the infusion of alien concepts have also let loose the forces of narrow national sentiment and ideologization of racial and cultural traditions, which are all brought to bear upon the deislamization process. Since language and thought are interconnected in their dependence upon each other, semantic confusion in the application of linguistic symbols brings about confusion and error in the interpretation of Islam itself and its worldview. An excellent example of this is the case of the infusion of Greek thought and philosophical problems into the Muslim mind through the writings of the Falāsifah. Al-Ghazzālī's refutation of them in his celebrated *Tahāfut al-Falāsifah* took into account precisely the same kind of problems relating to words and terms and concepts and their meanings within the context of Islam. But the present intellectual, cultural and spiritual crises among Muslims are considerably more serious than those caused by the Falāsifah and others in the past, as the fields of problems now cover almost every aspect of life, and not only the philosophical. Even our concept of religion is now confused by the infusion of alien concepts that have invaded the various disciplines encompassing the natural, applied, human and social sciences and the arts.

The rise of the Modernist movement in the latter half of the last century heralded not so much the emergence of a Muslim intellectual and spiritual awakening and sobriety; it marked, rather, the beginnings of a widespread and systematic undermining of past scholarship and its intellectual and spiritual leadership, leaving us to inherit today their legacy of cultural, intellectual and spiritual confusion. Respecting *tafsīr* and *ta'wīl,* for example, the founder of that movement and his immediate disciples consistently advocated methods whose character in fact approaches that of Christian hermeneutics, depending largely upon learned conjecture *(ẓann: ظن)* based on subjective speculation *(hawā: هوى)* and the notion of historical relativism. Although they included as a major part of their program the so-called renovation of the Arabic language, what has now in effect become more evident—*after* their revision and treatment of Islamic concepts couched in Arabic, and their assimilation of foreign concepts using Arabic terms and words to symbolize them—is indeed the need for such a renovation! It is true that in the past the Falāsifah and Muslim thinkers generally had to grapple with foreign concepts and find suitable Arabic words and terms to symbolize them without violating the forms of the Arabic words and terms and displacing their semantic roles in the Islamic conceptual system. But they in the past had withstood that supreme cultural and intellectual test. Today the Muslims and the Arabic language together with all other Islamic languages are forced to confront the same kind of test, albeit more intensive and of greater magnitude than in the past. *The difficulty of the problem is that it is not simply a matter of language, but a matter of worldview.* Semantic confusion as a result of misapplication of key concepts in the Islamic vocabulary can effect our perception of the Islamic worldview. Now the concept of education is one of the key concepts in the Islamic basic vocabulary. This is now connoted by the term *tarbiyah (تربية).*

The Concept of Education in Islam

It seems to me that the term *tarbiyah is* not quite precise nor yet a correct one for connoting *education* in the Islamic sense. Since it is of great importance that the term we use should convey the correct idea of education and of what the educational process involves, it is imperative that we now examine the term *tarbiyah* critically, and if necessary put forward a more precise and correct alternative. The meaning of education and of what it involves is of utmost importance in the formulation of a system of education and its implementation. Supposing I am asked: *What is educa-*

tion?, and I answer: *Education is a process of instilling something into human beings.* In this answer 'a process of instilling' refers to the method and the system by which what is called 'education' is gradually imparted; 'something' refers to the content of what is instilled; and 'human beings' refers to the recipient of both the process and the content. Now the answer given above already encompasses the three fundamental elements that constitute education: the process, the content, the recipient; but it is not yet a definition because those elements are deliberately left vague. Furthermore, the way of formulating the sentence meant to be developed into a definition as given above gives the impression that what is emphasized is the *process*. Supposing I reformulate the answer: *Education is something progressively instilled into man.* Now here we still encompass the three fundamental elements inherent in education, but the order of precedence as to the important element that constitutes education is now the *content* and not the *process*. Let us consider this last formulation and proceed in analysing the inherent concepts.

I shall begin with man, since the definition of man is already generally well known, and that is, that he is a 'rational animal'. Since rationality defines man, we must at least have some idea as to what 'rational' means, and we all agree that it refers to 'reason'. However, in Western intellectual history, the concept of *ratio* has undergone much controversy, and has become—at least from the Muslim point of view—problematic, for it has gradually become separated from the 'intellect' or *intellectus* in the process of secularization of ideas that coursed through the history of Western thought since the periods of the ancient Greeks and Romans. Muslim thinkers did not conceive of what is understood as *ratio* as something separate from what is understood as *intellectus;* they conceived the *'aql (عقل)* as an organic unity of both *ratio* and *intellectus.* Bearing this in mind, the Muslims defined man as *al-ḥayawān al-nāṭiq (الحيوان النّاطق)*,[9] where the term *nāṭiq* signifies 'rational'. Man is possessed of an

[9] See, for example, al-Jurjānī, op. cit., 39.

inner faculty that *formulates meaning* (i.e., *dhū nuṭq:* ذو نطق), [10] and this formulation of meaning, which involves judgment and discrimination and clarification, is what constitutes his 'rationality'. The terms *nāṭiq* and *nuṭq* are derived from a root that conveys the basic meaning of 'speech', in the sense of human speech, so that they both signify a certain *power* and *capacity* in man *to articulate words in meaningful pattern.* He is, as it were, a 'language animal', and the articulation of linguistic symbols into meaningful patterns is no other than the outward, visible and audible expression of the inner, unseen reality which we call *'aql.* The term *'aql* itself basically signifies a kind of 'binding' or 'withholding', so that in this respect *'aql* signifies an *innate property that binds and withholds objects of knowledge by means of words. 'Aql* is synonymous with *qalb* (قلب) in the same way as *qalb,* which is a spiritual organ of cognition called the 'heart', is synonymous with *'aql.*[11] The real nature of *'aql* is that it is a spiritual substance by which the rational soul *(al-nafs al-nāṭiqah:* النفس النّاطقة) recognizes and distinguishes truth from falsehood.[12] It is clear from this, and many more references which we have not mentioned, that the reality underlying the definition of man is this spiritual substance, which is indicated by everyone when they say "I". When we speak of education, therefore, it must pertain to this reality of man, and not simply to his body and his animal aspect.[13] In defining man as a rational animal, where we mean by 'rational' the capacity for understanding speech, and the power responsible for the formulation of meaning—which involves judgement, discrimination, distinction and clarification, and which has to do with the articulation of words or expressions in meaningful

10 See the article *al-nuṭq*, in al-Tahānawī, *Kashshāf Iṣṭilāḥāt al-Funūn,* 6 vols., Beirut, 1966, 6: 1418.

11 See Ibn Manẓūr, op. cit., vol. II, p. 457 col. 2, foll.

12 See further, al-Jurjānī, 157.

13 On the concept of man and the relation between his real substance, his animality and his body, see for example al-Tahānawī, article *al-insān,* vol. I, 75–78.

pattern—the meaning of 'meaning' in our present context, and based on the concept of *ma'nā* (معنى), is the *recognition of the place of anything in a system.* Such recognition occurs when the *relation* a thing has with other things in the system becomes *clarified* and *understood.* The relation describes a certain *order.* Meaning, conceived in the way I have formulated above, is a mental image in which a word or expression is applied to denote it. When that word or expression becomes an idea, or a notion, in the mind (*'aql* with reference to *nuṭq*) it is called the 'understood' (*mafhūm:* مفهوم). As an intelligible form that is formed in answer to the question "what is it?", it is called 'essence' (*māhiyyah:* ماهية). Considered as something that exists outside the mind, that is, objectively, it is called 'reality' (*ḥaqīqah:* حقيقة). Seen as a specific reality distinguished from the others, it is called 'individuality' or 'individual existence' (*huwiyyah:* هوية).[14] In this way and in the context of the present discussion we say that what constitutes meaning, or the definition of meaning, is *recognition of the place of anything in a system which occurs when the relation a thing has with others in the system becomes clarified and understood.* We say further that the relation describes a certain order. If every thing in any system were in the same place, then there could be no recognition, there could be no meaning, since there would be no relational criteria to judge, discriminate, distinguish and clarify. Indeed, there would be no 'system'. For recognition to be possible, there must be *specific difference,* there must be *essential relation* and, moreover, these must *remain,* for if the difference and the relation were not abiding but were in a state of constant change specifically and essentially, then recognition of things would be impossible, and meaning would perish. In this brief outline is already revealed the intrinsic connection between meaning and knowledge.

The second important element inherent in education is its *content,* which *is* here indicated as 'something'. This is done

---

[14] Consult, for example, al-Jurjānī, 235–236; and al-Tahānawī, 5: 1084–1085.

deliberately because even though we all know that it must refer to knowledge, we have still to determine what we mean by it. The teaching and learning of skills alone, however scientific, and no matter if what is taught and learned is encompassed in the general concept 'knowledge', does not necessarily constitute education. The teaching and learning of the human, natural and applied sciences alone does not constitute education in the sense we are clarifying. There is a 'something' in knowledge which if it is not inculcated will not make its teaching and learning and assimilation an education. In fact the 'something' that we allude to here is itself knowledge; indeed, it is knowledge of the *purpose* of seeking it. At this point we are compelled to ask: *What, then, is knowledge?* or: *What does knowledge consist of?* In the beginning, I referred to the fact that in accordance with Islamic tradition we understand definition as of two kinds: definition by *ḥadd* and definition by *rasm.* By the former is meant a precise or concise specification of the distinctive characteristic of a thing; and by the latter is meant a description of the nature of a thing. This distinction reveals that there are things which we can define specifically to its precise, distinctive characteristic—such as in the case of the definition of man—and there are things which we cannot so define, but can define only by describing its nature. Knowledge comes under this latter category. There are many definitions describing the nature of knowledge, but what is of relevance here is the epistemological definition, since it is important to understand what the Islamic epistemological context involves and implies. Perhaps its greatest implication lies in its effect upon our vision of reality and truth and our methodology of research, our intellectual scope and practical application in planning for what is called 'development', which all bear upon our understanding of education. Muslims are in concerted agreement that all knowledge comes from God, and we also know that the manner of its arrival, and the faculties and senses that receive and interpret it are distinctly not the same. Since all knowledge comes from God and is interpreted by the soul through its spiritual and physical faculties, it follows that the most suitable definition would be that knowledge, with reference to God as being its origin, is the *arrival (ḥuṣūl: حصول) in the soul of the meaning of a thing or an object of knowledge* (i.e., حصول معنى او صورة الشيء في النفس); and that with reference to the soul as being its interpreter, knowledge is the *arrival (wuṣūl: وصول) of the soul at the meaning of a thing or an object of knowledge* (i.e., وصول النفس الى معنى الشئ).[15] We have said earlier that the world of nature, as depicted in the Holy Qur'ān, is like a Great Open Book; and every detail therein, encompassing the farthest horizons and our very selves, is like a word in that Great Book that speaks to man about its Author.[16] Now the word as it really is, is a sign, a symbol; and to know it as it really is is to know what it stands for, what it symbolizes, what it means. To study the word as word, regarding it as if it had an independent reality of its own, is to miss the real point of studying it; for regarded as such it is no longer a sign or a symbol, as it is being made to point to itself, which is not what it really is. So in like manner is the study of nature, of any thing, any object of knowledge in Creation, pursued in order to attain knowledge of it; if the expression 'as it really is' is taken to mean its alleged independent reality, essentially and existentially, as if it were something ultimate and subsistent—then such study is devoid of real purpose, and the pursuit of knowledge becomes a deviation from the truth, which necessarily puts into question the validity of such knowledge. For *as it really is,* a thing or an object of knowledge is other than what it is, and that 'other' is what it *means. So* just as the study of words as *words* leads to deviation from the real truth underlying them, in the same way the preoccupation in philosophy with things as *things* leads to the erroneous, ordinary level of experience belief in the existence of their alleged essences outside the mind, whereas in reality the so-called *essences* are only mentally posited.[17] A thing, like a word, is in

---

15 See al-Jurjānī, 160–161.

16 E.g., سنريهم ايتنا في الآفاق وفي انفسهم حتى يتبين لهم انه الحق

17 I refer here the 'essentialist' view of reality as opposed to the existentialist view. By 'existentialist', however, I do not in our present discussion refer to recent Western philosophical speculation called

reality ultimately a sign or a symbol that is apparent and is inseparable from another thing not equally apparent, in such wise that when the former is perceived the other, which cannot be perceived and which is of one predicament as the former, is known. What we have outlined is in fact a summary exposition of the Quranic concept of *āyah* (آية) as referring to words and things.[18] That is why we have defined knowledge epistemologically as the arrival in the soul of the *meaning* of a thing, or the arrival of the soul at the *meaning* of a thing. The 'meaning of a thing' means the *right* meaning of it; and what is considered to be the 'right' meaning is in this context determined by the Islamic vision of reality and truth as projected by the Quranic conceptual system. We may now recall our earlier reference to the relevance obtained between *tafsīr* and *ta'wīl* as valid methods of approach to knowledge and scientific methodology respecting our study and interpretation of the world of nature, and its significance in our conception of knowledge and education. In the same way that *tafsīr* and *ta'wīl* apply to the Holy Qur'ān, involving its entire conceptual system, its reflected meanings in the *Ḥadīth* and Sunnah and in the things of the empirical world; so is the Book of the world of nature to be interpreted by scientific methods emulating those of *tafsīr* and *ta'wīl,* treating the things of the empirical world as 'words', as signs and symbols operating in a network of conceptual relations that altogether describe an organic unity reflecting the Holy Qur'ān itself. In this way also the Holy Qur'ān is the final authority that confirms the truth in our rational and empirical investigations. What we are saying is that knowledge, as referring to meaning, consists of the *recognition of the proper places of things in the order of creation, such that it leads to the recognition of the proper place of God in the order of being and existence.*

---

by that name, but to the Islamic view that existence (*wujūd*: وجود) constitutes the real essences of things.

18 For the meaning of *āyah* see, for example, Ibn Manẓūr op. cit., 14: 62, col. 1.

We said that there is a 'something' in knowledge which if it is not inculcated will not make its teaching and learning and assimilation an education. We said further that this 'something' is knowledge of the purpose of seeking it. Now when knowledge, which is here defined as recognition of the proper places of things in the order of creation, such that it leads to recognition of the proper place of God in the order of being and existence, is made the content of education, it still would not suffice to render the education an *education* in the sense we are clarifying—unless that 'something' in knowledge is included in the definition of knowledge. For *recognition* alone of the proper places of things and of God does not necessarily imply concomitant *action* on the part of man to behave in accordance with the suitable requirements of what is recognised. True recognition must be followed by acknowledgement, otherwise the recognition is in vain. Acknowledgement, like recognition, pertains to man and consists in man making himself suitable to the requirements of the right or proper places of things or affairs. The requirements of the proper places of things and affairs entail action on the part of man, and this action is denoted by the term *'amal (عمل)*. From this it is now clear that the 'something' in knowledge that we must have to realize education is *acknowledgement* of the proper places of things and of God that is recognized as existing in the order of creation and of being and existence. So now we are in a position to complete our definition of the content of education, as: *recognition and acknowledgement of the proper places of things in the order of creation, such that it leads to the recognition and acknowledgement of the proper place of God in the order of being and existence.*

In our definition of knowledge, that is, of what knowledge consists and of the content of education, we notice that the concept of 'proper place' pertains to two domains of application: on the one hand it refers to the ontological domain which includes man and the world of empirical things, and on the other to the theological domain which includes the religious and ethical aspects of human existence. 'Proper' place means 'real' and 'true' place as denoted by the term *ḥaqq (حق)*, for *ḥaqq* signifies both reality and truth pertaining to the two domains. *Ḥaqq* signifies a judgement or *ḥukm (حكم)* conforming with reality or the real situation. This judgment involves statements or uttered words or propositions, religious beliefs, religions and schools of thought. The exact opposite of *ḥaqq* is *bāṭil* (باطل), meaning falsehood, something vain, futile. The term *ḥaqq,* then, basically signifies a suitableness to the requirements of wisdom and justice.[19] We understand by 'justice' *('adl:عدل)* a harmonious condition of things being in their right or proper places. By 'wisdom' *(ḥikmah: حكمة)* we mean the knowledge given by God, by which the recipient is able to effect correct judgements as to the proper places of things. Thus when we speak of the truth of a matter as the suitableness of a fact or a reality to a judgment, we mean by that judgement that which is derived from wisdom. Truth or *ḥaqq* is then a *suitableness to the requirements of the proper places of things as recognized by true judgment.* The notion of right or proper places involves *necessity* for things to be in that condition, to be deployed in a certain order, arranged according to various 'levels' *(marātib: مراتب)* and 'degrees' *(darajāt:* درجات). Ontologically, things are already *so* arranged, but man, out of ignorance of the just order pervading all creation, makes alterations and confuses the places of things such that injustice occurs. When the truth of the matter is revealed to man and recognized by him, it then becomes incumbent upon him to guide his conduct so as to conform with that truth. By his conformity with that truth, he is in effect putting himself in *his* proper place. Recognition of the truth in both domains, the ontological and the theological, necessitates in man a conduct that conforms with that truth. Thus *ḥaqq* also signifies 'duty' or 'obligation' that binds in accordance with the requirements of reality and truth.[20] When in Islam we speak of

---

Confer al-Jurjānī, 94. See also al-Taftāzānī's commentary of the *'Aqīdah* of al-Nasafī, Cairo, 1335 A.H., 15–16.

20 A fuller treatment of the concepts of justice *('adl),* wisdom *(ḥikmah),* injustice *(ẓulm),* truth *(ṣidq),* untruth *(kidhb)* is to be found

man as possessing 'right(s)' in the sense of just claim or what he is entitled to, we mean by that his duty or obligation as described above. Thus 'acknowledgement' as the fundamental element in true 'recognition' in the Islamic concept of education means 'affirmation and confirmation' or 'realization' and 'actualization' in one's self of what is recognized. This is denoted by the term *taḥqīq* (تحقيق), which is derived from the same root as *ḥaqq*. Acknowledgement of what is recognized is what renders education an education; otherwise, recognition alone is but a 'learning' *(ta'allum:* تعلّم*)*.

At this stage of our exposition of the concept of education in Islam, we have already brought to bear upon it many of the key concepts that form the basic vocabulary of the Islamic conceptual system. We have briefly explained the concepts of meaning *(ma'nā)*; knowledge *('ilm)*; justice *('adl)*; wisdom *(ḥikmah)*; action *('amal)*; right or proper in respect of what is true and real *(ḥaqq)*; of reason *(nuṭq)*; self *(nafs)*; heart *(qalb)*; mind and intellect *('aql)*; hierarchical order in creation *(marātib* and *darajāt)*; words, signs and symbols *(āyāt)*; interpretation *(tafsīr* and *ta'wīl)*. We have woven these concepts together in meaningful pattern, elucidating the concept of education peculiar to Islam, which we now define as: *recognition and acknowledgement, progressively instilled into man, of the proper places of things in the order of creation, such that it leads to the recognition and acknowledgement of the proper place of God in the order of being and existence.* There is one other key concept which in reality is central to education and the educational process, because the others we have mentioned all focus their meanings in this context toward it alone, such that by itself it stands sufficient as the precise term to denote education. This is because the key concept alluded to identifies itself as the 'something' in knowledge which is knowledge of the purpose of seeking it. This major key concept is couched in the term *adab* (أدب).

---

in my *Islām: The Concept of Religion and the Foundation of Ethics and Morality*, Kuala Lumpur, 1976, 23–24, 25–27.

Adab is the discipline of body, mind and soul; the discipline that assures the recognition and acknowledgement of one's proper place in relation to one's physical, intellectual and spiritual capacities and potentials; the recognition and acknowledgement of the reality that knowledge and being are ordered hierarchically according to their various levels *(marātib)* and degrees *(darajāt).* Since *adab* refers to recognition and acknowledgement of the right and proper place, station, and condition in life, and to self-discipline in positive and willing participation in enacting one's role in accordance with that recognition and acknowledgement, its actualization in one and in society as a whole reflects the condition of justice *('adl).* Justice itself is a reflection of wisdom *(ḥikmah),* which we have already defined as that God-given knowledge which enables the recipient to discover the right and proper place for a thing or a being to be. The *condition* of being in the proper place is what we have called justice; and *adab* is the method of knowing by which we *actualize* the condition of being in the proper place. So *adab,* in the sense I am defining here, is also a reflection of wisdom; and with respect to society *adab is* the just order within it. *Adab,* concisely defined, is the *spectacle (mashhad:* مشهد*) of justice as it is reflected by wisdom.*

We said that *adab* identifies itself as knowledge of the purpose of seeking knowledge. The purpose of seeking knowledge in Islam is to inculcate goodness in man as man and individual self. The end of education in Islam is to produce a good man, and not—as in the case of Western civilization—to produce a good citizen. By 'good' in the concept of good man is meant precisely the man of *adab* in the sense here explained as encompassing the spiritual and material life of man. For man, before he became manifested as man, has sealed an individual covenant *(mīthāq:* ميثاق*)* collectively with God, and has recognized and acknowledged God as Lord *(al-rabb:* الرب*)* when he witnessed unto his self and affirmed 'Yea!' *(balā:* بلى*)* to God's 'Am I not your Lord?' *(alastu bi rabbikum:* الست بربكم*).*[21] This means that before he

---

21 7: 172.

assumed physical form man has been equipped with the faculty of spiritual cognition *(ma'rifah:* معرفة*)*, and was able to recognize and acknowledge, by the fact of what he said in affirmation (*qawl:* قول*)* through his intellectual power of speech *(nuṭq),* the reality and truth of his existential condition in relation to his Lord, that is, his Possessor, Creator, Sustainer, Cherisher, Provider. Indeed, this Covenant, and what it implies, is the very essence of religion *(al-dīn)* as enacted in Islam for all the principles of Islam ultimately revert to that spiritual, pre-existent condition.[22] So the men of spiritual discernment have referred to man in that spiritual condition as *al-nafs al-nāṭiqah*—the rational soul. The other aspect of man's nature is what refers to his manifestation in physical form: *al-nafs al-ḥayawāniyyah* (النفس الحيوانية)—the animal soul. Man then is a 'double associate'; a single being possessing a dual nature with two souls *(nafsān:* نفسان*)* analogous to it; the one higher in relation to the other. It is the recognition and acknowledgement by the lower animal self of its proper place in relation to the higher rational self that constitutes for that lower self its *adab.* 'Recognition' means discovering the proper place in relation to what is recognized; and acknowledgement means concomitant action *('amal)* resulting from discovering the proper place in relation to what is recognized. Recognition alone without acknowledgement is mere arrogance; for it is the *ḥaqq* of recognition to be acknowledged. Acknowledgement alone without recognition is mere ignorance; for it is the *ḥaqq* of acknowledgement to actualize recognition. Either one by itself is *bāṭil,* for in Islam there is no worthwhile knowledge without action accompanying it, nor worthwhile action without knowledge guiding it. The *just* man is he who effects such *adab* unto his self, resulting in his being a *good* man.

The concept of *adab* as I have formulated here is construed from its meaning as understood in the early, Islamic sense, before its restriction to the context revolving around the concept of

[22] See the work cited in note 20.

cultural refinement pertaining to letters and social etiquette, which was effected to a considerable extent by the innovations of the literary geniuses. In its original, basic sense, *adab* is the *inviting to a banquet.* The idea of a banquet implies that the host is a man of honour and prestige, and that many people are present; that the people who are present are those who, in the host's estimation, are deserving of the honour of the invitation, and they are therefore people of refined qualities and upbringing who are expected to behave as befits their station in speech, conduct and etiquette. The islamization of this basic concept of *adab* as an invitation to a banquet, together with all the conceptual implications inherent in it, which even then already involved knowledge, is significantly and profoundly expressed in a *ḥadīth* narrated by Ibn Mas'ūd, where the Holy Qur'ān itself is described as God's invitation to a banquet on earth, in which we are exhorted to partake of it by means of acquiring real knowledge of it (إن هذاالقرآن مادبة الله في الأرض فتعلموا مادبته).[23] The Holy Qur'ān is God's invitation to a spiritual banquet, and the acquiring of real knowledge of it is the partaking of the fine food in it. In the same sense that the enjoyment of fine food in a banquet is greatly enhanced by noble and gracious company, and that the food be partaken of in accordance with the rules of refined conduct, behaviour and etiquette, so is knowledge to be extolled and enjoyed, and approached by means of conduct as befits its lofty nature. Thus the men of discernment speak of that knowledge as the *food* and *life* of the soul; it is that which makes the soul alive. The *ta'wīl* interpreting the meaning of 'the living' *(al-ḥayy)* as 'the knowing' *(al-'ālim)* in the passage: 'He brings forth the living from the dead',[24] indeed refers to this knowledge as the food and life of the soul. Ultimately, real knowledge of it is the 'tasting of its flavour', the 'spiritual savouring' *(dhawq:* ذوق*)* that men of

---

23 *Ma'dabat* here means *mad'āt* (مدعات) see Ibn Manẓūr, 1: 206, col. 2. On the concept of islamization which I have introduced here, see above, 9–11.

See above, 5–6 and the references in note 7.

discernment speak of, which almost simultaneously unveils the reality and truth of the matter to the spiritual vision *(kashf: كشف).* In virtue of this, *adab* involves action to *discipline* the *mind* and *soul;* it is acquisition of the *good qualities* and *attributes* of mind and soul; it is to *perform* the *correct* as against the erroneous *action,* of *right* or *proper* as against *wrong;* it is the *preserving from disgrace.* Thus *adab* as the disciplinary action, the selective acquisition, the correct performance and the qualitative preservation, together with the knowledge that they involve, constitutes the actualization of the purpose of knowledge. When we say that the purpose of knowledge is to produce a good man, we do not mean that to produce a good society is not its purpose, for since society is composed of people, making every one or most of them good produces a good society. Education is the fabric of society. The emphasis on *adab* which includes *'amal* in education and the educational process is to ensure that *'ilm* is being put to good use in society. For this reason the sages, men of discernment and the learned scholars among the Muslims of earlier times combined *'ilm* with *'amal* and *adab,* and conceived their harmonious combination as education. Education is in fact *ta'dīb (تأديب),* for *adab* as here defined already involves both *'ilm* and *'amal.*

In the *ḥadīth* cited above, the conceptual connection between *'ilm* and *adab* is already established. In yet another, more well known *ḥadīth,* not only is the conceptual connection between the two concepts established in an even more direct way, but it is expressed in such a manner as to imply *identity* between *adab* and *'ilm.* The *ḥadīth* to which I refer is one in which the Holy Prophet, upon whom be peace, said: "My Lord educated me, and so made my education most excellent" (أدّبني ربي فأحسن تأديبي). The word I have translated as 'educated' is *addaba,* which according to Ibn Manẓūr, is synonymous with *'allama, (علّم)*[25] and which al-Zajjāj attributed to God's manner of teaching His Prophet.[26] The infinite noun of *addaba: ta'dīb,* which I have

[25] Op. cit., 1: 206, col. 2.
[26] Loc. cit.

translated as 'education', signifies the same, and we have its conceptual counterpart in the term *ta'līm (تعليم).* In our definition of meaning, we said that meaning is the *recognition of the place of anything in a system.*[27] Since knowledge consists of the arrival—in both senses, of *ḥuṣūl* and *wuṣūl*—of meaning in and by the soul, we defined knowledge as the *recognition of the proper places of things in the order of creation, such that it leads to the recognition of the proper place of God in the order of being and existence.*[28] In order to render knowledge an education we included the fundamental element of acknowledgement in the recognition, and we defined this content of education as the *recognition and acknowledgement of the proper places of things in the order of creation, such that it leads to the recognition and acknowledgement of the proper place of God in the order of being and existence.*[29] Then we defined education, including the educational process, as the *recognition and acknowledgement, progressively instilled into man, of the proper places of things in the order of creation, such that it leads to the recognition and acknowledgement of the proper place of God in the order of being and existence.*[30] Since meaning, knowledge and education pertain to man alone, and by extension to society, the recognition and acknowledgement of the proper places of things in the order of creation, must primarily apply to man's own recognition and acknowledgement of *his* proper place—that is, his station and condition in life in relation to his self, his family, his people, his community, his society—and to his self-discipline in actualizing within his self the recognition by the acknowledgement. This means that he must know his place in the human order, which must be understood as arranged hierarchically and legitimately into various degrees *(darajāt)* of excellence *based on the Quranic criteria of intelligence, knowledge,* and *virtue (iḥsān:* إحسان*),* and

27 See above, 15.
28 See above, 19.
29 See above, 20.
30 See above, 22.

must act concomitantly with the knowledge in a positive, commendable and praiseworthy manner. This self-recognition actualized in self-acknowledgement is the *adab* here defined. When we say that acknowledgement is the fundamental element in true recognition, and that acknowledgement of what is recognized is what renders education an education,[31] we are referring primarily to proper places in the human order, and in the order of knowledge and being. *Adab* is knowledge that preserves man from errors of judgement. *Adab* is *recognition and acknowledgement of the reality that knowledge and being are ordered hierarchically according to their various grades and degrees of rank, and of one's proper place in relation to that reality and to one's physical, intellectual and spiritual capacities and potentials.* In the light of the foregoing definitions and explanations, the words of the Holy Prophet, when he said: "My Lord educated me, and so made my education most excellent," may be paraphrased in the following way: "My Lord made me to recognize and acknowledge, by what (i.e., *adab*) He progressively instilled into me, the proper places of things in the order of creation, such that it led to my recognition and acknowledgement of His proper place in the order of being and existence; and by virtue of this He made my education most excellent." There should be neither doubt nor vacillation in accepting the proposition that the concept of education and the educational process is encompassed in the term *ta'dīb,* and that the correct term to denote 'education' in Islam is sufficiently expressed by it.

Tarbiyah, in its present connotation, is in my opinion a comparatively recent term, apparently coined by those who aligned themselves with Modernist thought. It is meant to convey the meaning of education without recourse to its precise nature. Now the Latin words *educare* and *educatio,* meaning in English 'educate' and 'education' respectively, are conceptually connected with Latin *educere,* or English 'educe': to bring out, to develop from latent or potential existence; in which the 'bringing out',

[31] See above, 21.

or the 'developing' process refers to physical and material things. The referents in the conception of education derived from the Latin concepts evolved from the above-mentioned terms encompass the animal species, and are not restricted only to 'rational animals'; and even though it may be conceded that intellectual and moral training are infused into the basic idea of education, they are not necessarily inherent in the basic terms themselves, and are an augmentation developed from philosophical speculation on ethics. Moreover, in spite of that, the intellectual and moral training referred to is itself geared to physical and material ends pertaining to secular man and his society and state. Those who coined the term *tarbiyah* to mean education were in reality reflecting the Western concept of 'education', for the term *tarbiyah,* in spite of what they still claim, is a transparent translation of 'education' in the Western sense, as the basic meanings conveyed by it are similar to those found in the Latin counterparts. Even though the advocates of *tarbiyah* continue to contend that the term is evolved from the Holy Qur'ān, their evolvement of it as such is based on mere conjecture, betraying their apparent unawareness of the semantic structures of the Quranic conceptual system. For semantically, the term *tarbiyah* is neither appropriate nor adequate in conveying the conception of education in the Islamic sense, as will be demonstrated in what follows.

In the first instance, the term *tarbiyah* understood in the sense of education as used today is not found in any of the great Arabic lexicons, some of which we mentioned at the beginning. Ibn Manẓūr did record the form *tarbiyah* together with several other forms from the roots *rabā (ربا)* and *rabba (رب)* as reported by al-Aṣma'ī, who said that they convey the same meaning. As to the meaning, al-Jawharī said that *tarbiyah,* and some of the other forms mentioned by al-Aṣma'ī, means to feed, to nourish, to nurture (i.q., from the root *ghadhā (غذا)* or *ghadhw (غذو)),* and this meaning refers to all things that grow, like children, plants and the like.[32] Basically *tarbiyah* means to nurture, to bear, to feed,

---

32 Ibn Manẓūr, 14: 307, col. 1.

foster, nourish, to cause to increase in growth, to rear, to bring forth mature produce, to domesticate. Its application in the Arabic language is not restricted to man alone, and its semantic fields extend to other species: to minerals, plants, and animals. One can refer to cattle farming and stock breeding, chicken farming and poultry husbandry, pisciculture and plant cultivation each as a form of *tarbiyah* respectively. Yet, as we pointed out earlier, education in the Islamic sense is something peculiar *only to man.* With reference to the rule of correct application of terms and concepts as illustrated by al-Jāḥiẓ in respect of *bukhl,* for example, the above point alone is sufficient to demonstrate that *tarbiyah,* being a term and concept applicable to many species and not restricted only to man, is not quite suitable to denote education in the Islamic sense, which applies to man alone. It is clear that the qualitative elements inherent in the Islamic concept of education and the activity or process involved are not the same as those involved in *tarbiyah.* Moreover, *tarbiyah* basically also refers to the idea of 'possession', such as the 'possession' of the offspring by their parents; and it is usually the possessor-parents who exercise *tarbiyah* on the relevant objects of possession, such as the offspring or others. The possession here meant is only of the relational kind, since true possession belongs to God alone, Who is the Creator, Nourisher, Sustainer, Provider, Cherisher and Possessor of All, which epithets and more are all encompassed and denoted by the single term *al-rabb.* Thus the word *rabba* and those derived from it denote, when applied to man and to animals, a 'borrowed possession', as it were. What they do with this borrowed possession is *tarbiyah* if what they do is nurturing, bearing, feeding, fostering, nourishing, rearing, causing to increase in growth, bringing forth mature produce, domesticating, and the like; it is certainly not educating if by education we mean primarily the inculcation of knowledge pertaining to man alone, and to man's intellect in particular. So when in order to conceive of *tarbiyah* as education we infuse into the term the essential meaning that conveys the fundamental element of knowledge, such infusion is artificial as the inherent meanings in the conceptual structure of *tarbiyah* do not naturally include knowledge as one of them. Now in the case of man it is usually the parents who exercise *tarbiyah* over their offspring, on account of the former's right of borrowed possession over the latter. When the exercise of *tarbiyah* conceived as education is transferred over to the state, there is danger that education becomes a secular exercise, which is what is happening in fact. This is so because the end of *tarbiyah* is normally physical and material and quantitative in character, as all the inherent concepts couched in the term pertain to physical and material growth and maturity only; and because the values set by the state are geared toward the production of good citizens—values which are naturally governed by utilitarian principles tending toward the physical and material aspects of man's social and political life. Yet we all know that the real essence of the educational process is set towards the goal pertaining to the intellect *('aql),* which inheres only in man. Since the essential intellectual element is not inherent in the concept of *tarbiyah,* the educational process that makes man recognize and acknowledge his position in relation to God, his true Possessor, and that makes him act in accordance with that recognition and acknowledgement, is in reality not a matter of *tarbiyah,* but a matter of *ta'dīb,* for *adab* towards God is but another expression of sincere servanthood as actualized in *'ibādah (عبادة).* So man's response to God's exercise of lording over him—of God's creating, nourishing, sustaining, providing, cherishing and possessing him—is *ta'dīb.*

In the second instance, and with reference to the argument that *tarbiyah* conceived as education is evolved from Quranic usage relating to the terms *rabā* and *rabba* conveying identical significations, what is said in the above paragraph already clarifies the pivotal point that the basic meanings of these terms—indeed ultimately on the authority of the Holy Qur'ān itself, as will now be demonstrated—do not naturally lend themselves to the essential elements of knowledge, intelligence, and virtue, which are really the constituent elements in true education. When we are exhorted by God to lower the wing of humility out of loving kindness to our parents, and say in supplication: My Lord! Bestow on them Thy Mercy as they have cherished me in childhood (واخفض لهما جناح الذّل من الرّحمة وقل ربّ ارحمهما كما ربّياني صغيرا)[33] the term *rabbayānī* there means *raḥmah,* signifying mercy or loving kindness. It refers to the feeding and loving and clothing and sheltering and nursing—in short the cherishing that parents bestow upon their children. In the passage: *irḥam humā ka mā rabbayānī ṣaghīrā,* the *ka* of *ka mā* is known as the *kāf al-tashbīh (كاف التّشبيه),* that is, the *kāf* of comparison, so called because of the similarity that exists between the concepts inherent in the words compared, which in this case refers to *irḥam humā (*i.e., to *raḥmah)* and *rabbayānī (*i.e., to *tarbiyah).* The literal meaning is: bestow on them mercy *like as when* they cherished me. *Tarbiyah* (the infinitive noun of *rabbaytuhu:* ربّيته) is like *raḥmah* or mercy. When it is God Who creates, nourishes, sustains, provides, cherishes and possesses, such acts, by which God is called *al-rabb,* are acts of *raḥmah* or mercy. When it is man who by analogy does similar acts to his offspring, it is called *tarbiyah.* Indeed, the primary signification of *al-rabb* is *al-tarbiyah,* meaning: the bringing a thing to a state of completion by degrees. But this bringing a thing to a state of completion by degrees as acts of *raḥmah*—and hence also by analogy as acts of *tarbiyah*—does not involve knowledge; it rather refers to an existential condition as distinct from knowledge. That *'ilm* or knowledge is distinct from *raḥmah* or mercy is evident from the Holy Qur'ān itself where it says that God encompasses all things in *raḥmah* and *'ilm* (وسعت كلّ شيئ رحمة وعلما).[34] In Islamic metaphysics, *raḥmah* signifies God's bestowing of existence *(wujūd)* to the creatures. Thus when we say that *tarbiyah* means bringing a thing to a state of completion by degrees, we understand the completion to refer more to the physical and material condition rather than to the rational and intellectual. The completion of the latter condition necessitates the inculcation of knowledge which, as we have shown, is not inherent in *tarbiyah.* So when Fir'awn said to the Prophet Mūsā, upon whom be peace: "Did we not cherish thee as

---

[33] 17: 24.
[34] 40: 7.

a child among us?" (الم نربك فينا وليدا),[35] we are not supposed to infer thereby that Fir'awn *educated* the Prophet, in spite of the fact that the former, from his use of the expression *nurabbika,* did exercise *tarbiyah* over the latter. *Tarbiyah* simply means cherishing, without necessarily including the inculcation of knowledge in the cherishing.

In the third instance, and even if it may be conceded that a meaning pertaining to knowledge can be infused into the concept of *rabba,* that meaning refers to the *possession* of knowledge and not to its *inculcation,* and hence it does not refer to education in the sense we mean. I am referring to the term *rabbānī* (رباني), the name given to wise men learned in the Knowledge of the Lord *(al-rabb).* Muḥammad al-Ḥanafiyyah is reported to have referred to Ibn 'Abbās as a *rabbānī* of the Ummah.[36] 'Alī ibn Abī Ṭālib is reported to have classified men into three grades, the first being the *'ālim rabbānī.*[37] Sībawayh said that the *alif* and the *nūn* in the term are added to indicate specialization in knowledge of the Lord to the exclusion of all other branches of knowledge.[38] Ibn al-Athīr said the same thing about the two letters being added to give intensiveness to the signification, and said further that the term is derived from *al-rabb* with the signification of *al-tarbiyah.*[39] However, according to Ibn 'Ubayd the term *rabbānī* is not really Arabic; it is either Hebrew or Syriac, and it is unknown to the Arabs, being known only to the jurists and men of science.[40] In the Holy Qur'ān three instances are found in which *rabbānī* is mentioned, and they all refer to the Jewish rabbis.[41]

---

35 26: 18.
36 Ibn Manẓūr, 1: 404, col. 1.
37 Loc. cit.
38 Op. cit., 403, col. 2.
39 Op. cit., 404, col. 1.
40 Loc. cit.
41 3: 79; 5: 47 and 66.

The Problem and its Solution

In the foregoing exposition we have analysed briefly the basic and relational significations of the terms *ta'dīb* and *tarbiyah;* and in that analysis we have clarified their distinctly different conceptual structures in order to determine their suitableness to the requirements of justice and wisdom, and to decide which is the more relevant, in defining education and the educational process within the context of Islam. We must now conclude that *tarbiyah* in its original signification, and in the way in which it was applied and understood by discerning Muslims of earlier times, did not and was not intended to denote either education or the educational process. The qualitative emphasis upon the concept of *tarbiyah* is mercy *(raḥmah)* rather than knowledge *('ilm);* whereas in the case of *ta'dīb* it is knowledge rather than mercy. *Ta'dīb* already includes within its conceptual structure the elements of knowledge *('ilm),* instruction *(ta'līm),* and good breeding *(tarbiyah),* so that there is no need to refer to the concept of education in Islam as *tarbiyah-ta'līm-ta'dīb* all together. *Ta'dīb* is then the precise and correct term to denote education in the Islamic sense. The consequence brought about by the relegation of the concept of *ta'dīb* as education and the educational process is the loss of *adab,* which implies loss of justice, which in turn betrays confusion and error in knowledge, which are all happening among Muslims today. In respect of the society and the Community, confusion and error in knowledge of Islam and the Islamic vision of reality and truth creates the condition which enables false leaders in all spheres of life to emerge and thrive, causing the condition of injustice *(ẓulm:* ظلم*).* They perpetuate this condition, since it ensures the continued emergence of leaders like them to replace them after they are gone, perpetuating their domination over the affairs of the Community. To put it briefly in their proper order, our present general dilemma is caused by:

1. Confusion and error in knowledge, creating the condition for:

2. Loss of *adab* within the Community. The condition arising out

of 1 and 2 is:

3. The rise of leaders who are not qualified for valid leadership of the Muslim Community; who do not possess the high moral, intellectual and spiritual standards required for Islamic leadership; who perpetuate the condition in 1 above, and ensure the continued control over the affairs of the Community by leaders like them who dominate in all fields.

All the above roots of our general dilemma are interdependent and operate in a vicious circle. But the chief cause is confusion and error in knowledge; and in order to break this vicious circle and remedy this grave problem, we must first come to grips with the problem of loss of *adab,* since no true knowledge can be instilled without the precondition of *adab* in the one who seeks it and to whom it is imparted. Loss of *adab* means the loss of the capacity for discernment of the right and proper places of things, resulting in the levelling of all to the same level; in the confusion of the order of nature as arranged according to their *marātib* and *darajāt;* in the undermining of legitimate authority; and in the inability to recognize and acknowledge right leadership in all spheres of life. The solution to this problem is to be found in education as a process of *ta'dīb.*

Of the problems intimately connected with the overriding one mentioned in the above paragraph is the problem concerning the concept of *adab* itself. The question may be raised as to why, if *adab* is central to education and the educational process, has *ta'dīb* not been discovered much earlier and applied as signifying education in the sense we mean here? The answer to this significant question is that we cannot truly say that *ta'dīb* meaning education and the educational process in the Islamic sense has not been discovered before, nor applied as such. On the contrary, there is every reason to believe that beginning from the earliest periods of Islam, *adab* became significantly involved in the emulation of the Sunnah of the Holy Prophet, upon whom be peace, and was conceptually fused together with *'ilm* and *'amal.* The earliest Muslims were told that the Holy Prophet was the embodiment of excellence in conduct such that he was and will continue to be the exemplar *par excellence*.[42] The Holy Prophet himself said, in the *ḥadīth* previously cited, that God instilled into him *adab* and thus made his *ta'dīb* most excellent. There is no reason to suppose that the earliest Muslims did not realize the significance of the *islamized* concept of *adab* as something to be evolved into education and the educational process characteristic of Islam. Indeed, historically, such movement is to be seen as already developing during the Umawī period, when *adab* was gradually conceived as encompassing the whole literature and culture of the Arabs. Then during the 'Abbāsī period, and with the islamization of a large part of the world, *adab* was further evolved to extend itself beyond Arab literature and culture to include the human sciences and disciplines of other Muslim peoples, notably the Persians, and even to draw into its ambit the literatures, sciences and philosophies of other civilizations such as the Indian and the Greek. But during the 'Abbāsī period also, the restriction of the islamized meaning of *adab*, which was in the process of unfolding itself, had begun—no doubt due, among other causes, to the urbanity that prevailed, and the attendant officialdom and bureaucracy. *Adab* became gradually restricted to *belles lettres* and professional and social etiquette. To this day this restricted meaning of *adab* is used, so that it is not surprising why the proponents of Modernist thought, as if unaware of the original significance of the concept of *adab* as an Islamic concept pertaining to education and the educational process, found it necessary to coin *tarbiyah* in place of *ta'dīb* and propagate its currency in the Muslim world. Almost a thousand years ago, al-Ghazzālī had already pointed out how the confusion in the Islamic sciences was caused by the *restriction* of the original meanings of terms to meanings not intended by the Muslims during the earliest periods of Islam. He listed five terms: *fiqh* (فقه), *'ilm*, *tawḥīd* (توحيد), *tadhkīr* (تذكير) and *ḥikmah*, that have earlier

[42] Q.v., the Holy Qur'ān, 33: 21—لقد كان لكم في رسول الله اسوة حسنة

been regarded as what he called the 'praiseworthy sciences', and that have in his time been conceptually tampered with so as to acquire restricted and changed meanings making them 'blameworthy'. *Fiqh* originally was intended to mean religious insight and discernment which brings about piety *(taqwā)*. In his time it was already restricted to mean jurisprudence. In the same way, the knowledge of God and of His Creation *('ilm)* was then also restricted to mean jurisprudence. *Tawḥīd,* which referred to the knowledge of spiritual reality and truth, became restricted to the science of dialectics *(kalām:* كلام*). Dhikr* and *tadhkīr,* which meant invocation and admonition respectively, were then changed to story-telling, the reciting of poems, esctatic utterances *(shaṭḥīyyāt:* شطحيات*)* and heresies. *Ḥikmah* and *ḥakīm* (حكيم) which referred to wisdom and to the wise, were then changed and restricted to refer to physicians, poets and astrologers.[43] Thus in the light of this cursory sketch of the conceptual history of the term *adab* analogous to what al-Ghazzālī said of semantic change and restriction with respect to certain other terms, the true answer to the question posed at the beginning of this paragraph is that the islamized concept of *adab* began from the beginning to translate itself significantly into the Islamic educational and scientific conceptual framework both in theory and in practice; but due to specific causes resulting from confusion and error in knowledge of Islam and the Islamic vision of reality and truth, it began to undergo a restriction of meaning which affected its role as a basic concept in the Islamic philosophy of education, such that in our times it is no longer understood in its original, Islamic sense, but in its restricted sense to the extent that *ta'dīb* is no longer recognized and acknowledged as meaning *education.*

With reference to what I said earlier in connection with the islamization of language, it is important to stress that semantic change in the islamized concepts are not to be attributed to what is vaguely called 'social change', but to ignorance and error

43 Al-Ghazzālī in the *Iḥyā'*, 1: 38–45 (Cairo, 1358, Muṣṭafā al-Bābī al-Ḥalabī).

which is productive of the confusion that *causes* social change. To say that such a phenomenon is caused by social change and to acquiesce to it as the exponents of modern linguistics teach is to imply the legitimacy of authority invested in society to effect semantic change. This kind of teaching is misleading and dangerous and must not be tolerated, for in Islam we cannot accept society as authoritative, or invest it with authority to bring about changes that will lead Muslims astray. Society, insofar as matters of knowledge and of the understanding of Islam and its worldview are concerned, has no authority; on the contrary, society is generally ignorant and needs proper education and constant guidance by the learned and the wise within it so as to ensure its salvation. On this matter, we may derive analogy from the Holy Qur'ān and reflect on what it says about the 'majority of men'—which refers also to 'society'; how they have no knowledge of the purpose of life and know only the external things of the life of the world; and how, if we follow their whims and fancies, they will lead us away from the Way of God.[44] This means that the learned and the wise among Muslims must exercise constant vigilance in detecting erroneous usage in language which impinges upon semantic change in major key concepts and creates general confusion and error in the understanding of Islam and of its worldview. We must also remember that the compilation of modern Arabic dictionaries and the initiation of journalistic writing among the Muslims have largely been the works of non-Muslim Arabs and orientalists. In view of this and of the considerable influence the dictionary and the newspaper have upon the thinking of the masses, the language and the currency of technical and other terms, and the propagation of alien concepts in the mind, we cannot afford to continue to allow confusion and error to creep surreptitiously into our cultural and intellectual life. Now, with regard to a major key concept such as that of education, three terms are currently applied to denote it in the Muslim world,

[44] See for example, 6: 115–6; 30: 6–7.

particularly in the Arab-speaking world, namely: *al-ta'līm* (التعليم), *al-tarbiyah* (التربية), and *al-ma'ārif* (المعارف). The fact that there is no unanimity in the use of a single term to denote such an important concept is itself succinct indication that the concept of education is not yet clarified in the minds of Muslims. Moreover, it indicates also that the term *tarbiyah* is by no means established in the Muslim world as a term which adequately expresses education and the educational process in the Islamic sense. We have here advocated the term *ta'dīb* instead, and consider it not untimely to propagate its use in order that we might reestablish its civilizing role in our intellectual and cultural history.

The Form of the System of Education in Islam

Each man is like a kingdom in miniature; a microcosmic representation (*'ālam ṣaghīr:* عالم صغير) of the macrocosmos (*al-'ālam al-kabīr:* العالم الكبير).[45] He is a dweller in his self's city (*madīnah:* مدينة) wherein is enacted his *dīn*. Since in Islam the purpose of seeking knowledge is ultimately to become a good man, as we have described, and not a good citizen of a secular state, the system of education must in Islam reflect man and not the state. The highest and most perfect embodiment of the educational system is the university; and since it is of the highest and most perfect systematization of knowledge designed to reflect the universal, it must also be a reflection not just of *any* man, but of the Universal or Perfect Man (*al-insān al-kāmil:* الانسان الكامل). The modern universities, which are based on Western models, do not reflect man, but rather reflect the secular state. This has been the case

---

45 The first Muslim thinker to formulate the idea, based on the Holy Qur'ān, that man is a microcosm reflecting the macrocosm was Ja'far al-Ṣādiq (d. 148). The idea was later developed by the Ikhwān al-Ṣafā and the Falāsifah, and it was established in the Islamic metaphysical system of the Ahl al-Taṣawwuf. For certain details about the idea, see al-Tahānawī in the article on *al-insān,* 1: 75–78; and *al-'ālam,* 4: 1055.

because there has never been in Western civilization—or in other civilizations apart from the Islamic—any Perfect Man who can become a model to emulate in life, and who can be made to project right knowledge and action in universal form as university. Only in Islam in the sacred person of the Holy Prophet, peace be upon him, is the Universal and Perfect Man realized. Since the concept of education in Islam pertains to man alone, its formulation as a system describes the model of man as perfected in the sacred person of the Holy Prophet. So the Islamic university must reflect the Holy Prophet in terms of knowledge and right action; and its function is to produce men and women resembling him as near as possible in quality, each one according to his inherent capacities and potentials; to produce *good* men and women; to produce men and women of *adab,* in emulation of him who said: "My Lord educated me, and so made my education most excellent."

Man is both soul and body; he is at once physical being and spirit; and his soul ought to govern his body as God governs the Universe. He is integrated as a unity, and by means of his interconnected spiritual and physical faculties and senses, he guides and maintains his life in this world. Just as man has a dual nature, so is knowledge of two kinds: the first, God-given; the second, acquired. In fact in Islam all knowledge comes from God, but the manner of its arrival as *ḥuṣūl* and *wuṣūl,* and the faculties and senses that receive and interpret it are distinctly not the same. Since the first kind of knowledge is absolutely essential for man's guidance and salvation, knowledge about it, which is comprised in the religious sciences, is necessary and obligatory to *all* Muslims *(farḍu 'ayn:* فرض عين*).* The acquisition of the second kind of knowledge, which includes the rational, intellectual and philosophical sciences, is obligatory to *some* Muslims only *(farḍu kifāyah:* فرض كفاية*).* The following cursory schemata of man, knowledge, and the university will clarify the corresponding relationships that obtain between them:

I MAN

1. His soul and inner being

(*rūḥ:* روح, *nafs:* نفس, *qalb:* قلب, *'aql:* عقل)

2. His body and physical faculties and senses

II KNOWLEDGE

1. The God-given knowledge
2. The acquired knowledge

III THE UNIVERSITY

1. The religious sciences *(farḍu 'ayn)*
2. The rational, intellectual and philosophical sciences *(farḍu kifāyah)*

When we superimpose the schema of knowledge on the schema of man, it becomes clear that the God-given knowledge refers to man's spiritual faculties and senses; while the acquired knowledge refers to his physical faculties and senses. His intellect *('aql)* is the connecting link between the physical and the spiritual, for the *'aql* is in reality a spiritual substance which enables man to understand spiritual reality and truth. In the same way, when we superimpose the schema of the university reflecting man on those of knowledge and man, it becomes clear that the religious sciences represent the *farḍu 'ayn* knowledge at the core of the university which, like man's soul, is the university's permanent and abiding center, and embodies the highest expression and systematization of what is obligatory to all Muslims. What has generally been understood to this day of the concept of *farḍu 'ayn* is the restricted form composed of a static formula taught in the childhood stage of life and limited only to bare essentials. What must be understood by that concept is its original meaning and intention; that such knowledge is fluid and increases in scope and content as one increases in maturity and responsibility, and according to one's capacities and potentials. So in the tertiary system of education the *farḍu 'ayn* knowledge is to be taught not only at the primary level, but at the secondary and pre-university and university levels also, the scope and content designed in gradations each as befitting each level. But the scope and content at the university level must *first* be formulated before they can be projected in successively lesser gradations to the lower levels, for the university level represents the highest and most complete formulation and systematization; and only when that is achieved can they become the model for the rest. Otherwise, if we commence with attempting the formulation of its scope and content from the lower levels, we shall never succeed, as no perfect and complete model of the highest order is available to serve as the criterion for the formulation of their scope and content. The core knowledge representing the *farḍu 'ayn,* integrated and composed as a harmonious unity at the university level as a model structure for the lower levels, and which must invariably be reflected in successively simpler forms at the pre-university, secondary and primary levels of the educational system throughout the Muslim world, must reflect not only the Sunnī understanding of it, but also accommodate the Shī'ī interpretation. The division of the two kinds of knowledge may be briefly summarized as follows:

I THE RELIGIOUS SCIENCES

1. The Holy Qur'ān: its recitation, and interpretation *(tafsīr* and *ta'wīl)*
2. The Sunnah (السنّة), the life of the Holy Prophet; the history and message of the Prophets before him; the *ḥadīth* and its authoritative transmission
3. The *Sharī'ah (الشريعة):* jurisprudence and law; the principles and practice of Islam *(islām:* اسلام; *īmān:* ايمان; *iḥsān:* إحسان*)*
4. Theology: God, His Essence, Attributes and Names and Acts *(al-tawḥīd:* التّوحيد*)*
5. Islamic metaphysics *(al-taṣawwuf:* التّصوّف*)*; psychology, cosmology and ontology; legitimate elements of Islamic philosophy including valid cosmological doctrines pertaining to the hierarchy of being
6. Linguistic sciences: Arabic, its grammar, lexicography and literature

II THE RATIONAL, INTELLECTUAL AND PHILOSOPHICAL SCIENCES

1. The human sciences

2. The natural sciences
3. The applied sciences
4. Technological sciences

With respect to the rational, intellectual and philosophical sciences, each branch must be imbued with Islamic elements and key concepts *after* the foreign elements and key concepts have been isolated from its every branch. This process constitutes its *islamization*. The islamization of knowledge means the deliverance of knowledge from its interpretations based on secular ideology; and from meanings and expressions of the secular.[46] The isolation of the foreign elements from every branch of this knowledge refers mainly to the human sciences, although it must be noted that even in the natural and applied sciences—particularly where they deal with interpretation of facts and formulation of theories—the same process of isolation should be applied. To this knowledge must be added new disciplines relating to:

1. Comparative religion from the Islamic point of view.
2. Western culture and civilization. These must be designed as a means for Muslims to understand Islam in relation to other religions, cultures and civilizations—particularly that culture and civilization that has been, is, and will continue to be confronting Islam.
3. Linguistic sciences: Islamic languages—grammar, lexicography and literature.
4. Islamic history: Islamic thought, culture and civilization; the development of the sciences in Islam; the Islamic philosophy of science; Islam as world history.

These new disciplines, particularly 4 above, will ensure logical continuity and cohesion in the successive educational progression from the religious sciences to the rational, intellectual and philo-

---

[46] See my *Islām and Secularism*, Kuala Lumpur, 1978, chapters I, II and V.

sophical sciences and vice versa.

What I have briefly outlined above of the division of knowledge and the classification of the sciences, is no more than an evolvement of ideas firmly rooted in the Muslim religious and intellectual tradition. We know that from the earliest periods of Islam, Muslim thinkers have repeatedly made attempts to classify the sciences, and their various classifications were successively increased in scope and content with the increase in knowledge.[47] But the division of knowledge into two seems to have begun from the very beginning. At the same time the harmonious unity of the two kinds of knowledge has always been emphasized and maintained. No single branch of knowledge ought to be pursued indefinitely exclusively of others, for that would result in

---

[47] A classification based on the Aristotelian model was set forth by al-Kindī (d. c. 257). Al-Fārābī (d. 339) accomplished a more elaborate classification, adding into it the Islamic disciplines. Ibn Sīnā (d. 428), al-Ghazzālī (d. 505), and Ibn Rushd (d. 596) were all influenced by al-Fārābī in their respective classifications, and they made some modification and elaboration, as did the Ikhwān al-Ṣafā (4th century) who came after al-Fārābī. Ibn Khaldūn's (d. 809) classification and analysis reflected what was established of the division and description of the sciences in the Muslim world up to his period. An idea of the division of the sciences as known in the 12th century of the Islamic era can be seen in al-Tahānawī, 1: 4–53. See also *The Metaphysics of Avicenna* (New York 1973, translated from the Persian with commentary and critical analysis by Parviz Morewedge) of Ibn Sīnā's *Dānish Nāma-i 'Alā'ī*, the first chapter on the number of the philosophical sciences; the *Rasā'il* of the Ikhwān al-Ṣafā, Dār Ṣādir, Bayrūt [n.d.], 4 vols., 1: 266–275; *The Muqaddimah: An Introduction to History* of Ibn Khaldūn, translated from the Arabic by F. Rosenthal, New York, 1958, 3 vols., vols. 2 and 3, ch. VI, pp. 436 foll. Summaries on the divisions of the sciences by al-Fārābī, the Ikhwān al-Ṣafā, and Ibn Khaldūn are also found in Seyyed Hossein Nasr's *An Introduction to Islamic Cosmological Doctrines,* Mass., 1964, 40–43; *Science and Civilization in Islam,* New York, 1970, 60–65.

disharmony, which would affect the unity of knowledge, and render its validity questionable. This standpoint, which is consistent with, and indeed characteristic of the Islamic religious and intellectual tradition, means that although the Islamic university that we envisage must provide for specialization in particular branches of the rational, intellectual and philosophical sciences, and even in the religious sciences themselves, the concept of *specialization* will not convey the same meaning in the Islamic educational context as the term generally means today. Specialization does indeed refer to the needs of society and the state; but as we now see it, specialization does not necessarily have to realize what it signifies to a secular state and society. Closely connected with this, the very structure of the university itself will have to be different from what is generally known in practice. The priorities, powers, functions and deployment of the faculties and departments within it, as well as its administration, will also not be similar to what is existing in practice; for if the university were to reflect the Universal and Perfect Man, then its external and internal structures, its government and maintenance, its recognition and acknowledgement of right authority within itself will all have to be a functioning imitation of the schema of man as envisaged in Islam. Due to the many implications involved, we must be bold enough to experiment with the creation of a *new* university, and not seek to change existing ones.

Finally, with reference to the rational, intellectual and philosophical sciences, and to the isolation of foreign elements and key concepts that have been infused into them, the foreign elements and key concepts are to be identified as originating from Western religious and intellectual tradition, and they are:

1. The concept of dualism which encompasses their vision of reality and truth.
2. Their dualism of mind and body; their separation of *intellectus* and *ratio,* and their stress upon the validity of *ratio;* their methodological cleavage pertaining to rationalism and empiricism.
3. Their doctrine of humanism; the secular ideology.

4. Their concept of tragedy—mainly in literature.

The isolation of these key concepts from every branch of the rational, intellectual and philosophical sciences is its islamization. Islamization is the *liberation of man first from magical, mythological, animistic, national-cultural tradition, and then from secular control over his reason and his language.* The islamization of language brings about the islamization of thought and reason. Deislamization is the infusion of alien concepts into the minds of Muslims, where they remain and influence thought and reasoning. It is the causing of forgetfulness of Islam and of the Muslim's duty to God and to His Messenger, which is the real duty assigned to his true self; and hence it is also injustice to the self. It is tenacious adherence to pre-islamic beliefs and superstitions, and obstinate pride and ideologization of one's own pre-islamic cultural traditions; or it is also secularization.

Petaling Jaya
Rabīʿ al-Ākhir 1400
1 March 1980

والله اعلم بالصواب

والحمد لله رب العالمين

والصلاة والسلام على اشرف المرسلين

وعلى اله واصحابه والتابعين

لهم باحسان الى يوم الدين

أمين

LIST OF ISTAC PUBLICATIONS

WORKS OF SYED MUHAMMAD NAQUIB AL-ATTAS IN ENGLISH

Comments on the Re-Examination of Al-Rānīrī's Ḥujjatu'l Ṣiddīq: A Refutation (Kuala Lumpur Museum Department) (1975)

The Correct Date of the Terengganu Inscription (Kuala Lumpur Museum Department: First Edition 1970) (1984)

The Oldest Known Malay Manuscript: A 16th Century Malay Translation of the 'Aqā'id of al-Nasafī (1988)

Islām and the Philosophy of Science (1989)

The Nature of Man and the Psychology of the Human Soul (1990)

On Quiddity and Essence (1990)

The Intuition of Existence (1990)

The Concept of Religion and the Foundation of Ethics and Morality (1992)

Islām and Secularism (Second Impression; First Impression 1978) (1993)

The Meaning and Experience of Happiness in Islām (1993)

The Degrees of Existence (1994)

Prolegomena to the Metaphysics of Islām: An Exposition of the Fundamental Elements of the Worldview of Islām (1995)

The Concept of Education in Islām (ABIM: First Impression 1980) (1998)

WORKS OF SYED MUHAMMAD NAQUIB AL-ATTAS—TRANSLATIONS

Ḥaqīqat al-Sa'ādah wa Ma'nāhā fī'l-Islām (The Meaning and Experience of Happiness in Islam) (1995)

Darāmadī bar Jahānshināsi-yi Islāmī (Preliminary Discourse on the Metaphysics of Islam: An Introduction to the Worldview of Islām) (1995)

Islām va Dunyāvigari (Islām and Secularism) (1996)

Mafhūm al-Ta'līm fil-Islām Iṭār Taṣawwurī li-Falsafah Islāmiyyah li-al-Ta'līm (The Concept of Education in Islām) (1998)

Die Bedeutung und das Erleben von Glückseligkeit im Islām (The Meaning and Experience of Happiness in Islām) (1998)

BOOKS ON ISLAMIC SCIENCE

Hamarneh, S. K., *Directory of Historians of Islamic Medicine and Allied Sciences* (1995)

Açıkgenç, Alparslan, *Islamic Science: Towards a Definition* (1996)

Badri, Malik, *The Aids Crisis: An Islamic Socio-Cultural Perspective* (1997)

Akdoğan, Cemil, *Albert's Refutation of the Extramission Theory of Vision and His Defence of the Intromission Theory* (1998)

BOOKS ON ISLAMIC THOUGHT

Açıkgenç, Alparslan, *Being and Existence in Ṣadrā and Heidegger: A Comparative Ontology* (1993)

Al-Attas, Syed Muhammad Naquib, *Prolegomena to the Metaphysics of Islām: An Exposition of the Fundamental Elements of the Worldview of Islām* (1995)

Cerić, Mustafa, *Roots of Synthetic Theology in Islām: A Study of the Theology of Abū Manṣūr al-Māturīdī (d. 333/944)* (1995)

Ceylan, Yasin, *Theology and Tafsīr in the Major Works of Fakhr al-Dīn al-Rāzī* (1996)

Kuşpınar, Bilal, *Ismā'īl Anḳaravī on the Illuminative Philosophy —His İẓāḥu'l-Ḥikem: Its Edition and Analysis in Comparison with Dawwānī's Shawākil al-Ḥūr, Together with the Translation of Suhrawardī's Ḥayākil al-Nūr* (1996)

BOOKS ON JURISPRUDENCE/LAW

Moussavi, Ahmad Kazemi, *Religious Authority in Shi'ite Islam: From the Office of Mufti to the Institution of Marja'* (1996)

Al-Ma'sumi, Muhammad Saghir Hassan, *Ibn Ḥazm's al-Risālah al-Bāhirah (The Magnificent Epistle) (Translated for the first time with an Introduction and Notes)* (1996)

Mustafa Mahmoud Abu-Sway (ed.), *The Fatāwā of Imam al-Ghazzālī (450–505 A.H./1058–1111 C.E.)* (Critically Edited with Introductions and Notes) (1997)

OTHERS

Wan Mohd Nor Wan Daud, *The Beacon on the Crest of a Hill: A Brief History and Philosophy of ISTAC* (1991)

Commemorative Volume on the Conferment of the Al-Ghazālī Chair of Islamic Thought on Prof. Dr. Syed Muhammad Naquib al-Attas (1994)

Al-Attas, Sharifah Shifa (ed.), *Proceedings of the Inaugural Symposium on Islām and the Challenge of Modernity: Historical and Contemporary Contexts, Kuala Lumpur, August 1–5, 1994* (1996)

BOOKS IN ARABIC

Mohaghegh, Mehdi (ed.), *The Kitāb al-Shukūk 'alā Jālīnūs of Muḥammad Ibn Zakariyyā al-Rāzī* (1993)

Nasr, S. H., Mohaghegh, M. (eds.), *Al-As'ilah wa'l-Ajwibah: Questions & Answers by Al-Bīrūnī and Ibn Sīnā* (1995)

Dibaji, Ibrahim (ed.), *The Kitāb Bayān al-Ḥaqq bi Ḍiman al-Ṣidq by Abū al-'Abbās Faḍl Ibn Muḥammad al-Lawkarī* (1995)

Ḥaqīqat al-Sa'adah wa Ma'nāhā fī'l-Islām (The Meaning and Experience of Happiness in Islām—Arabic translation; trans. Hassan El-Nagar) (1995)

Al-Zahrāwī, *Kitāb al-Taṣrīf li man 'Ajiza 'an al-Ta'līf* (On Surgery and Instruments) (eds. and trans. Ahmad Aram, Mehdi Mohaghegh) (1996)

Ibn al-Jazzār al-Qayrawānī, *Ṭibb al-Fuqarā' wa'l-Masākīn* (ed. Wajihah Kazim Al-i Tu'mah) (1996)

Dibaji, Ibrahim (ed.), *Kitāb al-Manāhij fī'l-Manṭiq* (1997)

Hāmed Nājī Isfahānī (ed.), *Sharḥ Kitāb al-Qabasāt—A Commentary on Mīr Dāmād's Kitāb al-Qabasāt* (1997)

Al-Attas, Syed Muhammad Naquib, *Mafhūm al-Ta'līm fil-Islām Iṭār Taṣawwurī li-Falsafah Islāmiyyah li-al-Ta'līm* (The Concept of Education in Islām) (trans. Hassan El-Nagar) (1998)

BOOKS IN PERSIAN

Darāmadī bar Jahānshināsi-yi Islāmī (Preliminary Discourse on the Metaphysics of Islām by Syed Muhammad Naquib al-Attas—Persian translation) (1995)

Islām va Dunyāvigari (Islām and Secularism—Persian translation by Ahmad Aram) (1996)

The Degrees Of Existence (Persian translation by J. Mujtabari) (1996)

Chahārumīn Bīst Guftār (The Fourth Collection of Twenty Treatises on Persian Literature, Islamic Philosophy, Theology and History of Science, by Mehdi Mohaghegh) (1997)

ISTAC MASTER'S THESES SERIES

Zainal Abidin Baqir, *The Problem of Definition in Islamic Logic* (1998)

AL-SHAJARAH (BIANNUAL JOURNAL OF ISTAC)

Volume 1 (1996)

Volume 2 (1997)

Volume 3 (1998)

INTERNATIONAL INSTITUTE OF ISLAMIC THOUGHT
AND CIVILIZATION (ISTAC),
205A JALAN DAMANSARA, DAMANSARA HEIGHTS,
50480 KUALA LUMPUR
Tel: 603-254 4444 Fax: 603-254 8343
E-Mails: istac@po.jaring.my (administration); aistac@po.jaring.my (academic); listac@po.jaring.my (library); istcssa@po.jaring.my (publications)

9 788119 024025

Printed at Repro India Ltd.